As Landscape

Mark Weiss

As Landscape

chax press
2010

ISBN 978 0925904 76 8

Chax Press
411 N 7th Ave Ste 103
Tucson AZ 85705-8388
USA

Parts of this book have been published in the journals *Fulcrum* and *Shearsman*, and as the chapbook *Figures: 32 Poems* (Tucson: Chax Press, 2001).

Printed in Canada by Friesens.

CONTENTS

I. Numbers: 16 Poems

I

He sees her urgent face.

.

Lakes folded into the palm of the hills.

.

Large two-legged passersby.

.

Sky gods
earth gods
gods of the air
legions of angels.

.

In the land
where everyone does everything backwards.

II

Imagine the moon between its arms
like the sky, or
the down on a woman's legs. There's
a cactus here, a kind of
prickly pear with down where the spines should be.
Hand
full of tiny spines.

III

The black spot on the dove's neck.
The ill-favored son of the loveliest of men.
The tough lyricist
the desert dancer
barefoot among the cactus.

.

Quiet. Slow.
Serpent-knowledge in the hollows of rocks.

IV

Cast a dark shadow
on a hot street.

.

In the dark
imagine water.
Fill the night
with trees.

In a dry place
sagebrush and cactus.

.

A haphazard life
defined by shadows.

.

The farm a wasteland.

A sense of entitlement
as vast as all outdoors.

.

Strata upon strata, and by the river
a deer nuzzles a mule. "Talks" to.

.

The smell of horses.
The smell of oats.

.

Whole forests reduced to toothpicks.

.

The legendary rage
against the implacable machine.

Still holds.
Leave little mark
behind you.

Each piece
builds the edifice.
Look what I found.

V

A man spits   big wad
clear across the subway tracks. Anyway,
something to be proud of.

VI

Frost on the road
eye on the goal.

Lost in the snow
like a big baby.
.

Forget what I know.

The language impoverished by forethought.

In a mute country
shards of thought.
The brilliance of sea-creatures.
.

The mute within the sounding brass
the silence
at the heart
of all traffic.
.

The bull
runs blindly to his death   no compromise in him
for his tormentors.
Bewildered, furious
and dead. This has nothing
to do with me, as if to say,
the wrong address,
the holy cause.

While spring cast blossoms on the pear
she spilled her music
into every cup.

Knowledge
is the engine
and the pursuit.

There is a seed of sorrow,
a plant at rest
beneath.

.

Still up at 4 a.m.
to write
to paint.
A bird
improbably
prepares for dawn,
a query
before sleep.

I had set out to make stars
and made a snarl.

VII

Sits down
leans back against the wall
and points her toes like a dancer.

VIII

Boyish.
lithe.
"A new man,
and *this* one
wears sox."

.

A fairytale through which the river flowed.

.

Floating in some sort of viscous medium.

.

In his grief
their presence
tore him apart.

.

What did I know of the lost provinces?
That was my father's time.

.

Loose in her clothing   poised
so that only her toe

.

He thinks the women
will want his hands on them
pulling them towards him.

.

The bride of randomness.

Reading by stormlight.

Testing the darkness
as if stepping off.

.

Immolation of small creatures on a light bulb.
Slave and master.
The trivialization of everyday life.
Only the noise of the waves to guide him.

.

A dance for the virgin.

The rise and fall of breath
as delicate as the ocean.

IX

What do you know
of other places?

That I drink from this well.

.

Something of the passion for seeing.

Finding.
Underfoot, the beach
littered with
the purple gonads of jellyfish.

Gathered starfish all the day and at night
saw all the stars of Orion.

X

Ten gulls stare out to sea. Handful of shards of the
unimaginable.

.

Warm stone.

.

Dead warbler on the porch.

.

The harmless life that nobody leads.

XI

I close my eyes and the god Chac
comes to me,
powerful as the sun.

All pleats and finery.

.

His apples.
Her breasts.

.

The transformative process at play.

.

Having become
the unquiet spirit
you always feared I would.

.

"I hate
carrying the virtuous
with a rancorous heart,"
she said.

.

Always surprised at whatever I've
found there.

.

. I wished it, and it
happened.

.

I was a bird
I was a lamb
I was a man.

.

"Took the wrong
step, walked into
another rhetoric."

XII

What falls
makes time.

All of this has its consequence. A sequence of trees   threes
noses   threnodies.

Salty flower

The poor at the gates.

On the empty canal a gull.
A snake.

Holds up her veil.

Pried
like a clam
from its solitude.

Even the process invisible.

Let me lead you
down that garden path.

XIII

Smelling of books and the sea   rusty
salt crusted.
Upturned dories seagulls the town
haphazard beyond the washlines
nets   gulls   shriek
and parry
old fish-guts   an island
a cloud   an island
a cloud.

XIV

The great swale of the boat's wake
across the calm bay.
The figure receding
then lost.

Horsetail clouds
the moon's ghost
flat water.
In the face of sentiment
grown mute.

XV
DISGUISES

Relentless mobility.

.

Expensive dress that
her body rejects
even as she wears it. Too
sweaty, or
uneasy, a different kind of grace,
a different animal, as if a dog were constrained
to live as a cat. Or a
social thing,
no other choice,
she thinks.
But she wants to be naked, even here, with everyone watching.

.

Carefully placing
each foot, as if
the sidewalk were a precipice.

.

Wouldn't that be a swamp to fall into.

.

She had lost the other hand as a teenager,
waving impetuously before boarding the plane,
a friend's one-engine prop on a fun hop to the next town. She
          didn't notice
the turning propeller. Sheared off
at the wrist. After that
she wore a store-mannequin's hand,
much like her own,
except that the nails
were always perfect.

XVI

In a tour of the body
discovering the most hidden, least discussed
formations of flesh and cartilage.

.

A fold
here and there
distinctive as fingerprints.

II. Figures: 32 Poems

I

Clean sneakers, and
a calculating mind.
"I wanted to write a paper on the
German Expressionists" she said "have you ever been
really stoned?" and went on
in that vein.

II

The waitress rubs her nose.
She wishes there were someone to talk to
in that whole crowd of clatterers.
She shifts her weight,
leans an elbow on the bar,
rests her head.
Translucent ears. When she
stands with her back to the light
pink
to their deepest whorl.

III

A dog and its echo roar in the mountains.

.

Startled birds explode from the grass
beside the high water that floods
the field by the small house in the woods.

.

Facing the wind at the top of the ridge
and other fierce pleasures.

.

A license to wonder.

.

A white gull shakes a pizza crust
from a paper bag.

.

I don't like his things in the apartment–bones, etc.

.

In a dream I was writing a long
poem on a tattered, loose-woven shred
of something, leaning,
I think, on a shoulder blade. In the dream I woke up too tired
to write it down, and lost it.

IV

The god who rests at noon in the shade of the fig tree, who loves
the dark-eyed girls.

Women
smelling each other's wrists
as a form of greeting.

The girl whose only skill was attracting boys.

Grateful for the small breeze.
Watching the light move across the shadow.

V

How do I know when you touch the cat
that you feel as I feel.
Suppose that you said "I love the feel
of its fur like strands of glass its icy touch as it cuts
sharp channels across the thin shells
of my fingers."

VI

Big dipper spread across the north
Jupiter overhead
Mars above Red Hill just clears
the treetops. So many stars
in the lake. Cold. A dog
barks somewhere, echoes across the valley. A chorus of echoes.
And one loon slices the night.
.

Anything from a chipmunk to a bear
or a human intruder. The dogs
all night alert.

VII

Morning's sharp shadow out my eastern window and the sharp
        shadow of the toothy fence across the way   last night's
        rainwater on the pool covers
clothes billowing and the toss
of the last golden leaves of the maples.

A cloudless
windy sky a
wind-scrubbed sky.

VIII

My father prowls the house.
No hope for the fearful animals.

IX

A last only
streak of magenta through a gray
cloud bank to the south
where the windows face   a cold
comfort, a poor excuse for sunset. And this morning
on the window ledge   a lone
pigeon   the pink
ridge of its beak, its hard
precise nostrils.

X

A nice place
for twilight to descend,
despite the cross. *Ach! do'*
hengst du, as my grandmother
used to say, in the familiar, one Jew
to another, as if to say, my,
aren't you everywhere today.

XI

A gull
shakes one foot
then the other
scratches its neck
and resumes its dignity.

XII

It's a cow
because it has horns.
We call the dewlapped cow
a moose.

XIII

The fat man bestrides the world.

.

Old Man Saguaro
down the canyon.

.

The hum of blood   the stream
the one fly.

.

The sun, just a glow
over the mountains to the west,
lights each detail of the mountains to the east.
The mountains to the west in flat, smoky, purple shadow.

.

The neighbor's daughter has long blond legs and a way
of getting off her bicycle.

.

Wind from the west
where the sun went down
and the weather
tonight
will come from. Like the wind
blew it over.

.

A dim peach streetlight
the one
with palm fronds
blowing behind it
and the sky above the mountains
an ochre line.

.

Sitting in a garden chair
in the middle of a concrete path through scrubby grass
stocking-footed
watching the place where the sun
went down. A perky blond,
blood-red shirt and jeans,
walks past, out the neighbor's door,
and gets in her date's blue car.

Chilly. Chill
dusty wind,
the grit
clear from California.
And what do you call these other trees,
the feathery,
cottonwoods?

XIV

On the table
a mound of raw cotton–thistly stems and oil-seeds–and a spray
of desert broom
that's blossomed,
though plucked
this indoor week, and now
on the first breeze of an open doorway
will fill the room with pollen.

XV

He sees her urgent face.
It must be late.

Oh, cat
made a mess, kibbles
all over the place.

XVI

Layers of sand and snow beige
white
beige
on the windy beach. Have I
said that before
beige white beige
and the blowing spume
have I   sky
scrubbed blue and the scud
of high cirrus   beige
white   blue and white
and the rusty sound of a gull the creak of wing the ghost of a plover
the ghost of summer in the cold rasp of their hovering.
Unimaginably cold water to plunge to for a bit of fish.

XVII

The hierarchy of poverty between those with shoes and those
     without
and those with the ingenuity to make shelter out of a piece of old
     plastic.

XVIII

All the banal junk that
floats through your head. Cheese on rye, lox and
cream cheese. A sense
of what I was supposed to be doing
all this time.

.

Attacked by the format.

.

You have never asked it the right questions.
For the sake of, for the sake
of?
An old man beneath a blossoming pear tree. An old man
covered with pear blossoms an old man
covered with leaves an old
man in a field of weeds an
old man in
snowtime. He was sliding
his white feet across the ice like
skittles, a fringe of hair and a dirty robe,
a dust of snow
at the edge of the pond. Pine trees
black as crow feathers.
There was a swing, I think, a weathered board
hung from a tree,
and a large stone, granite,
a few crude garnets, the sheen of mica.

.

A dark place beneath the trees.

Hair the color of ashes.

.

Every tendon quivering.

In the midst of pain
the return of eloquence.

.

Ambition overflowing
beyond the lingerie.

.

You hold the towel in both hands,
Beth said,
and wipe your ass. That's
dancing.

XIX

Landscaping with a torch.

.

Moving towards silence,
refractive darkness.

.

Just the artifacts,
nothin' but the artifacts.

The rush
of memory

green grow

the wind blowing.

.

The generous weight
smell of bread, of breast
the taste of nipple blood
nerve and skin
and the blood nerve
and skin of lips.

The several small gates of the body
holding it in,
keeping it out.

.

Shoe mimics foot,
glove   hand.

.

Whistles two times and speaks
three languages.

Disengaged from language.
Colors denoting
politics
not flowers.
My white anger.
My black anger.

.

couplet-congress
triplet-long weekend
quatrain-olympics
cinquaine-the French presidency
sextet-senate
septet-sanctuary
octet-the limits of power
nonet-a bad fall
decade-decade
eleven-or seven
twelve-boxcar

.

Taking another look.
Having decided all the important questions he said
hosanna, hosanna
was all he had left
to say.

.

Shows me
her awkwardness, to draw
towards her, her weight.

.

To search out the woman
behind the mother.

.

Suddenly without options
no place to say

.

Dismayed   glazed   gray-eyed   splayed.

XX

1

The young scholar talks with her date
about the reproductive rates of women.
Everyone's important, she says, how thin
can you spread yourself?

.

A smile, with the edge of a grimace.   ·

.

"You're like
a light bulb when he walks up," she said,
and then, "I'm sorry, that's a
terrible image."

.

Popcorn and sperm all over the bed.

.

The northern lights
over the prow of the mountain.

.

Are and were,
not will-be.

The master of thighs.

A health tour to the working class.

To complete the record.

.

Wasted much time.

Ate anything.

2
Legs crossed, and a shoe
dangling.
More the *idea* of woman.

.

A particular way of holding herself that says "little girl."

.

The inflection that says
"quotation"
the cast of hips
the cast of eyes
hand as guide to foot.

.

Less and less reveals the life I know.

3
Those with the automatic gestures
those with the permanent scowl
those bent those backward-footed.

XXI

Eat the baby
spit out the bones

filling the hollow space with life.

Long carpals and metacarpals the last
joint of her left
thumb, for instance, when her hand
shields the near side of her face
in shyness.

.

The pleasure of watching an obvious strategy.

.

Each day each night I
thrust and parry
carry the voice and the
the bag of and

that breathless language.

.

A beauty that her mother never had.

.

Potted plants old flowers
coffee grounds
punctuation   depiction
narrative.
The nature of the fluid calligraphy of light
through the slits of the blinds
onto gauze curtains
shimmering

in every breeze
from every viewpoint.

.

The defense of modesty is the maker's
scant integrity.

.

Because you couldn't
be other than you are.

.

As through gauze curtains
the dance of impatience.

XXII

The dialects of laughter.

The dialects of dogs and cats.

Attention wanders. He trims his beard   imagines
alternate bone structures based on a new
catalogue of surgical
choices.
.

The forms of formlessness,
Springtime a set of lines or dots.
.

Smell of dog food from the kitchen, and the orange
pom-pom girl on the tube
across the bar.
"Get real,"
we say.

XXIII

A child's dream of grace.
In the marketplace.
A flight of finches into the cottonwood. Mountains
through the archway.

XXIV
PAINTED

She had got used to addressing the servants in her own language.

.

Raucous laughter
opaque as the Chinese magazine I bought today
for the pictures of naked women. On the bar
branches of cherry blossoms.

.

Tattoo of heels.

.

Stepin Fetchit in whiskers.

.

A labor dispute among the reindeer.

.

Hunting the celebrity trophy   Bambi
Rudolph   Dumbo.

.

Society is all but rude
To this delicious solitude.

.

All you can eat.

.

In the midst of great happiness
listen to the voice inside you crying
'desist, desist.'

.

Swan-luminous night.

.

Golden
as a crust of bread.

The smell of grapes.
Lost
amid vine-clad.
.

A careful man
dips his brush   the tip
a cone of black. .
.

Like a swan's neck.
.

She thought that motherhood was a fine thing she thought
that children should be seen and not heard she
thought that children should have their
heads shaved, their
own world, a bathtub, a
doubtful plaything. She
paid attention to her friends' children she thought it
fine for a child to bite the dog she was an
unripe fig, a
flower, an
unbroken seed.
.

A gesture, as if
suddenly naked, had discovered
her nakedness   the hand
between them shielding her face.
Floats into his arms as if the air
were liquid.

Body hunger
found and lost

repeats and repeats
and finally comforted. Look,
the storm
is what saves, the bed
a sort of cradle.

.

Riding my bike through the dogwoods   busts
of poets in "blind rapture,"
girls in white, pulled by
dogs, fragile
as a bough of blossoms.

.

At the band shell
cameras,
small girls in leotards,
small comforts,
dreams of grace.

.

Dip the brush lightly,
just the tip,
come away pink
and touch the paper.

.

Embracing sleep itself.

.

A place with songbirds.

XXV

A woman stands watching the waves. For hours
she stands watching them, her bare legs
reflected in the wet sand.
From time to time she kneels
into the retreating water,
harvests
something.

XXVI

Some sort of weird distortion. In the distance
under the mist
gulls on the beach the size of turkeys. A heat mirage. The air
wavers, the truck on the sand
appears to skate on water.

.

A red-bellied bug
some kind of beetle
a scant quarter inch
of determined motion. And before,
a moth? Black wings
white spots
each of its legs orange,
swollen with pollen.

.

A running figure of a woman
against the fog
in the hard sand by the water.
Scatters the gulls,
herds them towards me.
Stops.
Picks up what she's dropped.
Straightens
runs again
assumes definition
white maillot
tan skin
dark hair
full breasts.
The tide retreating.
All manner of flotsam.

Another woman, stately as a Tuareg,
walks past me as I hunt for shells. She wraps
her towel as a sarong
around her hips. I'm naked.
We nod, and she continues
into the fog.

.

Down on my haunches to piss in the sand.
Then bury the water.

.

Pauses
on the edge of invisibility.

.

A solemn fog. The other body,
also naked,
the color of sand.

.

The sun, through mist, as strange as moonlight.
A swift
dives toward the bushes.

.

Piss again   the warmth
coursing through and out, a mound of sand
a comforting pressure
behind my scrotum.
The waves like footsteps to my left.

XXVII

"My country,
Romania,
take,
cut finger. One finger
first time, next finger
next time.
Very hard ruler
two, three hundred year."

XXVIII

A last drink with the boatman
and the water lapping. Lost
in blue froth
at the edge
of the wave at the end
of night.
Layers of froth, and inland
the sound of dawn birds and the last revelers.
Wind blows the white pages.
Last blue of night
first blue of morning.

.

The dangerous conflict
of the nonhuman.

.

Into the darkest place
the light penetrates.

Sculpting with light.

The ghost of a brush stroke
the ghost of a thought
the ghost of an imprint.

The shore of the sun
the powder of light

and at night

here on the edge of it
here where it breaks or drifts

this vulgar place
density of event
dots in a matrix.

The sail   the sun
the horizon.

.

Sky interpenetrates the tree
as an act of passion.

.

Skytheater.

.

The bend of a thumb
the bend of a nipple.

.

The thrilling rain.

.

Someone has died in this thrilling rain.

The terrible wind in
whatever kind of trees.

.

I have made this voyage
before,
and before
and before

and before.

XXIX

The bad times inflaming
all the casual hatreds.

.

Chitchat at the end of the empire.
Nostalgia as a political program.

.

These are the three-toed fossil prints
where a pigeon walked across concrete.

XXX

Howling with the dog.
.

The development of the motiveless line.

An uninflected commentary.

Radically affective,
the color red
the ground ochre
here and there a few green things.
Happened that way, like
a flash in the dice-cup.
.

The one
with the ring
in her nose.
.

From the ordinary utterance.

Le mot juste falls into place
like broken glass.

The cry of the siren
the cry of death in the street
the cry in the night.

The lessons of shadows
an *s* like the flight of birds.
.

A question of cartilage.
.

The visible structure of water.

.

Who's to draw the sums of courage?

.

An astringent music.

.

Saying, not singing.

.

Imagining his daughter's wet panties. His daughter in split panties
like a moral judgement.

.

A small boy's tyranny.
A stained little girl.

.

The science of noses would begin with
a system of classification.

.

To study:
the nature of change and the illusion of permanence.

.

Pelican plop,
stun fish.

.

They don't think like us.

.

Conversations in turquoise and aqua.

.

My toes   those poor
cowering things.

.

Awaiting the cohesive principle
along with the rest.

.

Clack clack of palm fronds in a high wind.

XXXI

From the darkness of sensual Europe
the ebullient anthropologist
applauds like a seal.

XXXII
FOR BASHŌ

Frog jumps in.

You hadda be there.

III. Elegies: 12 Poems

I
PARADOX

The stone mason's tink like an insistent bird
distinct against the gray wash of traffic.

.

To begin the whole
complex business again.

.

Killed the cat,
but nonetheless

Killed the cat
scared a rat
ate the hat
ground the bat.

.

You will lose a finger
but it won't be yours
you will have a baby
with many toes.
          The earthquake
will split the ground you
have nothing to do with.

.

Takes it in his hand and
drops it upwards.
Leaves a shadow.

II

Elected girl least likely to wear panties
when she meets
her in-laws for the first time.

III

Bone-Smasher, that tooth, is gone, and
Grinder, his friend.

IV

Temporary lives in the tidal slough
where the bar has become a long
slice of sand parallel to the beach
four feet away, glazed by the wash
of the receding tide's slow froth (the water on the bar
as silver and quick as a school of alewives).
There is a need for continuity of purpose,
a study beyond the instant.
The moon tilts
like a rakish hat, those dry
lava planes called
"seas" clearly visible above the horizon. A crow flies eastward.
      In the distance
children, dogs.

V
ELEGY

Let us now
vilify the dead
for being dead.

.

The swirl of tide across the beach.

.

The inevitable war between mammals and flies.

.

Love is an anger.
Random as pigeons.

.

He   he   he   he
the sound of laughter
I   I   I
the gulls' cry
we   we   we   we
that little piggy that falling water.

VI

The drowning man's thirst.

.

Building a structure out of moments of clarity.

.

Let's imagine ourselves through this one.

.

To heal the schism.

.

As if to demand of the listener
the light streaming through the high clerestories,
the mechanical squeak of a gull's wing. To deny clouds
to deny gray flowers
to deny all colors. I say
the lips the hair
the purple iris.

VII

Said nothing. Slipped a knife
between his ribs.

.

The war to end time.

.

What you want
is a strenuous analysis
of the simple
act
the doe
forming
its cheek
to the man's
hand.
The fact:
her face molded
to the man's hand
the geometry of passion
for all practical
purposes endless.

.

Had to climb a wall
to get here.

VIII

Turned like a
sunflower to
face him.

To watch
your awkwardness
ungainly leg
across the bulwark.

IX

The mythic event of entry into the earth
made banal by the proliferation of tunnels. I know
what the hill hides, what's under
the hill.

X
ON GREAT SOUTH BAY

All day the night-chill
nestles beneath the eaves
waiting for darkness.

.

The sun seems to hang in the sky.

.

Any source of joy.

.

Underfoot, the weathered terrain of old boards.
Squeak of two trees
rubbing their branches.

.

34 swans on Great South Bay,
a dozen baymen, and
one white sail. Sharp steady breeze
southerly, off the ocean,
sun to the south.
Wind-blown sumac.

.

Because a fire was in my head.

.

Low sun through the thicket of overgrown sumac.
Now 46 swans on Great South Bay
feeding and preening and
spreading their wings to the last light.

.

And then
the dark passion
intrudes upon sunlight, my heart

aches and a
drowsy numbness,
or worse, the stalker that
battens on happiness.

.

And I built him a bower in my breast.

.

Very quietly trying to change things.

XI

Fierce wind off the land   the waves
trailing manes of spray behind them,
so that they become great
white horses in a frenzy
to climb the beach, their hooves
tossing huge scoops of sand behind them, into the path
of the next horses.

XII

Sun come down as if the sea
sucked it under
like an egg.

IV. From Darkest Europe

BEGINS AND ENDS WITH BLOOD

Turned a stony eye on all beggars.

Rumbles of the old heroic fustion.

.

Things to eat and wear.

.

Salty flower.

Become a part of the shadow.

.

Came upon a cluster of Jewish graves. One monument over each family vault. Among the Jewish stones an occasional discreet cross on the marble slab covering the vault of a branch of a converted family that chose, nonetheless, to be buried among its own. On the slabs—lists of those buried, many with military honors from the first and second world wars, followed by "and to the memory of..." and a list of those whose bodies never came back. Two elderly parents, and a middle-aged daughter "who chose to follow her parents," "slaughtered together on the same day at Auschwitz." A family of three, two parents and a twenty year old, a medical student, arrested by the Germans, year of birth given, but after the customary dash a blank. "They never returned." Families, from 80 year olds to infants, "killed by the Germans at Auschwitz." I saw the names of the very old who died just before the war, and thought how lucky they were for their timely deaths.

The lists on many graves were truncated: deaths to 1940, none until the 50's, because, of course, there were no bodies.

"I had not thought that death had undone so many" came back insistently and repeatedly, as a mantra to help me fight through that thicket of well-tended stones. These were my dead, and I sensed

93

that I knew them: the pride in their assimilation, their status as bourgeois—you could see it in the quality of the stones and the list of achievements, the discreet differences from their Christian neighbors—their fur-collared coats, the smell of their cooking, the fierce familial attachments. Their terror when the gestapo came, and on the train across Europe, faced with the gas chamber. The Dreyfus family was among them—no mention of his peculiar history, but lots of others with military careers, military deaths—and one very young man dead at Auschwitz.

I wrote them an epitaph:

> neither a sudden death
> nor a death prepared for.

.

The poor at the gates.
What did you lose there?

A landscape of missing parts.

"...when they burnt the books."

"What else can you do but move inwards, don't
we all," he
says.

Memory   as refuge

and the dream
the scream in the night.

Ate rats,
got shot.

"What we all experience."

.

Two thieves,
the bold
and the sneak.

.

Nine stories above where the cold earth
thickens the air. Not far from here
on the empty canal a gull.

A gull.
A snake   a fish.

.

Holds up her veil.

.

Pried
like a clam
from his solitude.

.

On the Mexican figurine
a flower of blood where the bullet struck.

.

Sharp flutter of wings in the gray courtyard
and the wings of the wash in the windows
and the wondering child.

.

Through gray clouds, blue.
A clothes-rack
projecting from the window
speaks the life within. A woman
smiles at a child
and works too hard,
washing by hand
after the week's wages. The man

takes a break, drinks coffee
at the small table across from the sink,
enjoys a still moment. The smells of old soap
and hair. For the child
the small apartment and its shabby courtyard
are huge, luxurious with mystery.

.

Somewhere in waistcoats
a handful of economic forces.

.

The tears and laughter
the ordinary boredom and anxiety
the cleaning, the washing
the bathing
smells of food   hunger
surfeit
the hum of talk
the plotting of strategies.

The inaudible hum in the throat
in the lungs
the negotiations
between strangers
the questionings
the smells of sweat
sperm
rot
mildew
soap
turnips
beer
leather
the old in walkers
the caretakers

the people with dirty nails
the market-workers at work since 5
the immigrants
working their eyes out.
At noon
bowing in the streets towards a distant
concentration of wealth and power
and the streets of the living filled with the dead, beds filled with
        lovers and the memories of lovers
those who work too hard and those who can't work at all
those who make and those who squander
those who look those who see
those who question and those who don't
those who write
those who paint
those who stretch supper
those who study for the love of study
those who clean pipes fix cars make it work
those who exercise and those
dying of exhaustion
those in veils
those naked
those who welcome
those who scorn
those who loose the bonds.
Sky, sky
high wind and gray clouds
ragged wings
scurry of feet
building and breaking
noise in the street, and
a quiet courtyard.
And beyond
the dream of space
the dream of green

the dream of white.

.

No easy ideologies.

.

A chosen privation.

.

Cold rain begins to streak the windows.
A stroke of lightening.

.

Outside the net
outside the act of.

Not what is, but
what must be.

Not about, but
driven by.

Lapidary.

The bud
cut, blood welling
to the glass.

FROM DARKEST EUROPE

1
Having been treated to industrial slaughter
hard not to sympathize with the animals. My Christian girlfriend
in admiration
calls me her 'beast.'

Like a bird
taking off,
she said.

The slaughter-house at Auschwitz
the cannibal feast
imagination of same.

*En tout cas   les conditions de boucherie ne sont pas aussi mauvais
qu'aux camps, mademoiselle.*

Humble food served well
to pass the time in exile.

Certainly it's the distribution of goodies that's failed.
Devours its children.

2
The higher up the food chain
the better.
Stupid to be born a cow,
if one had the choice.

"Lovely hand   deft bones
little meat."

.

So long in the tub that her flesh
seemed ready to come off the bone.

.

Ritual slaughter.

3
No landscape shrugs off history
but hides the scars.
A school for despair
a school for anger
a school for burn and build.

.

The faint
comforting smell
of his own excrement.

.

Not to spend a lifetime
carving a stone.

4
Image of the *shtarke*   my grandmother's
legs like columns.
What a dance that was.
When my grandmother was seven her mother died
and they fled Poland. When she was twelve
her father killed himself.
Alone, then,
until the final bitterness of marriage.
Proud as a cactus.
Six months before her death
I held her naked body for the doctors to look at, surprised
at the fleshliness, the softness
of her old skin. Over and over she asked me

if the rent were paid. Over and over   as if to be homeless
and old.

As if to be dead.
.

In the midst of what's silent.
.

How do you live with the weight of compassion.

V. A Provisional Poetics

I never set out to write a poem. I will jot things down in my notebook, sometimes ideational, sometimes not, sometimes picked up from the environment, or misheard, or from a dream, and occasionally a phrase will have a rhythmic urgency that compels me to jot something further, and then I'm lost in process and have no idea where I or the poem is going. This is a liminal state fraught with both joy and terror, and it is processual. The process may extend over few or many lines and take a few moments or days and months. It lasts until one emerges at the other end, back into the everyday, arrival signaled by the loss of urgency.

And then one cleans up the mess of blind alleys, dishonesties and false starts. What's left is the record of the process. in which the poet is reinvented and the poem discovered.

What I'm describing is a particular form of possession. I think of poor Yeats in "Among School Children," realizing that, despite the watchful eyes of the nuns and his desperate desire to behave properly, he is falling into a sexual revery about a little girl. And suddenly he gives into the revery and finds himself transported to a brutal figuration of generativity and destructiveness, of the erotic refusing to be tamed to the appropriate. The life built by the public man can be torn apart in a second, and the whole world with it. It's Red Hanrahan, the hero of his early stories, carried off by the fairies all over again, a victim of their purity of impulse. And where does that leave you?

I suspect that all poetry is a form of possession. There's the sense that no matter how we try to train ourselves we can become at best receptive—the poem seems to come when it wants to and to leave when it wants to, unless we try to constrain it to our preconceptions, in which case we certainly lose it. And it's no respecter of occasions, so that those who have the dubious fortune of being on the receiving end often find themselves less than well-fitted to the world in which time-constraints are appropriate.

I'm not talking about a loss of choice. For one thing, the field in which our possessed selves operates is the field we bring to the experience. And the momentary changes and impulses are directed by what comes before, but also by the changes in a bodily chemistry whose stability is always fragile. We learn, we enlarge the field, but it's still the field, and the physiology, we brought to the game.

Even when we sleep we make choices. On the crudest level, it's no accident that Freudians have Freudian dreams, Jungians have Jungian dreams, and pharaohs dream about sheaves of grain. What we relinquish is the conscious awareness and direction of choice.

Rituals, whether parlor-game tarot readings or the I Ching or the more serious commitment of the otherwise decorous old woman in a New York or Havana neighborhood who becomes the horse of Shango and insists on throwing up her skirts to show the crowd how much bigger her cock is than theirs, are about choices faced in what Van Gennep called a liminal or marginal state—between statuses, in transit from known to knowable, a place without rules. The known and the knowable are always under siege, because it's not so much that we're on occasion in a stable place as that the rate of change on occasion slows down. Change is the constant. The poem is situated in that awareness, and to the extent that we have the courage to stay there it inhabits the liminal, which is by its nature formless. And the poem grounds itself in the particular because that's all there is to hold onto, and the only clues offered.

It's the willful relinquishing of resistance to liminality. And it differs from the ritual practice of possession because, unlike the ritual, which, if done properly, always brings the participant out the other end (imagery of rebirth is inevitable here), it has no preordained pattern, no life-rope, no social structures surrounding it that announce when the participant has reached the new place and what place that is.

This may sound like the fugue state of psychosis, but in fact the crazy rarely will themselves to relinquish the inhibitions to behaviors seen as crazy and to the internal states that drive those behaviors. They really know that they may not be able to come back. I once asked a group of for-the-moment stable schizophrenics about a fantasy. They exchanged a few panicky glances and then assured me, one after the other, in the manner of well-behaved school-children, that they didn't have fantasies.

Somewhere the poet has the sense that there's an internal structure to escape to, and it's that faith that gives him the courage to dive in when he's able. Yeats, for instance, knows that he's not about to throw himself on that little girl, although he may allow himself to court the danger. The internalized self-definition as Poet, which contains within it the privilege to depart from the everyday to bring back news from the margins, is a part of that structure.

Here's how I've been making poems these last fifteen years.

For a period of three years, from 1981 thru July 1983, I experienced seizures, on average four days a week, as many as four in one day. They were what is called partial seizures—a kind of petit mal—which in my case took the form of bizarre internal language events followed by a half hour of aphasia. Although they were no fun they had their comic side: in the first phase if anyone spoke to me I would hear his speech as ironic use of psychobabble. At first this seemed appropriate, if unusual—the first several occurrences happened while talking to my students, all psychology majors, in office hours after a psychology course I was teaching. When Carlos, my step-son, then thirteen, did the psychobabble routine I thought, my, he's become sophisticated. Then a Chinese waiter did it while taking my order, and then a singer on a salsa jukebox in a Puerto Rican greasy spoon.

The effect, more from the antispasmodics than the seizures, was that whereas previously I had written mostly self-contained work with something like a beginning, middle and end I could no longer sustain the linguistic energy—the best that I could do was fragments in my notebook. I thought my life as a poet was over. Then, on a drive across country, I began to realize that there was something magical happening—the fragments across time were not only forming their own fragile coherence, but they were more fully expressing all of my concerns and something like a shadow-sketch of the world as I experienced it. Parts of my way of being and seeing, notably irony, found themselves included in ways they hadn't been before, along with ideas, shopping lists, linguistic and cultural detritus. When I got to Tucson I spent an afternoon reading to a friend from my notebook. In the act I realized that I was involved in the process of a long poem occasioned by the crossing.

I think I'm engaged in what I understand as composition by field. Or perhaps composition of field. The field defines the observer, much as the light space around a darker mass creates the sense of depth in painting. The observer—the poet—becomes he who saw/

selected these things and not others from the limitless world, and chaos becomes information. In this way of writing it's rarely necessary to announce one's emotional states or even one's politics. The posited field and the data it contains comment in themselves, much like the data in dreams. A psychologized "no ideas but in things?"

Subsequently I have realized that much of what I had done for the previous twenty years had been moving in this direction.

Jerry Rothenberg likes to say that collage is the dominant art form of the twentieth century.

Which leads to another story:

Carlos was six years old when we first met. We used to take long walks together in our neighborhood. I was, and am, in the habit of picking up odd pieces of junk on the street, evaluating them, and sticking those I liked in my pocket for later display. I'm particularly fond of rust and gunk—a fine patina, as it were. Carlos would look up at me with an expression that seemed to say, "This guy is really a freak, I wonder if he's dangerous. Mom's taste in men, after all...," and I would explain to him what I thought was wonderful about the particular rusty bolt that had lost its cap or the small hieratic flange from an obscure car part. Pretty soon he'd be scouring the street, picking up objects for me to evaluate, and I would give a detailed critique of each bit of broken glass or twisted wire. Then one day he came home dragging behind him the deliciously ruinous and filthy exhaust system of a car.—eight feet of it. His mother froze with horror, but I was bursting with pride, although, in order to preserve the domestic tranquility, I had to tell him that, while it was a great, indeed monumental, find, it would be best if he restricted himself

109

to smaller objects. That was the moment that I realized I had been teaching Carlos to violate the first rule of Mommydom: you don't pick things up off the street. I wasn't aware that I was being subversive, although it seems obvious to me now that he and I were building an alliance out of the forbidden. I had, unconsciously, been training him not only in "art appreciation," in seeing the object as form divorced from function, but in the appreciation of detail and in the improvisatory construction of realities out of referents from different, often warring, systems. True bricolage, very close to the term's proletarian origins.

There are moments when the familiar object is seen with particular clarity, like a child seeing for the first time, and the words come forth spontaneously, simultaneous to and at the speed of perception. Cassirer in *Word and Symbol* describes the formation of language as the unlooked-for discovery of a series of what he calls "momentary gods," the cthonic deities whose presence makes certain places sacred. Each of those places, he thinks, may be the site where object and sound appeared simultaneously. Named at the moment seen. Preintellective. This, to use Blake's terminology, is the pole of innocence, the child's perceptual moment and burst of surprise. The pole of immediacy. And I try to write from that pole. But there is also the inescapable pole of experience, the adult's memory of object and word, the awareness that self and object are never more than for a moment apparently stable, that birth, death, and change inhere in all things. So the experience is always double: the simplicity of first perception and the ironizing presence of personal and tribal history.

It may be easier to understand this in terms of visual art. Here's an easy explanation of abstraction. I can imagine a perfect found object, a stone or a seashell. Then I can imagine making something that self-contained. This is good as far as it goes, but of course I'm describing only one kind of abstraction. What describes Brancusi's practice doesn't do at all for Pollock. If Brancusi is creating perfect stones Pollock is creating undreamt-of organic networks. And each is working, given their goals, as succinctly as possible, so that the observing eye and mind has a chance to hold the experience for a moment and understand.

One looks at the world as new, trying to avoid the ironies of sentimentality, golden ages and such, and one looks at it as experienced, caught in the web of connectivities. At a point in my work, aware of having reached a limit, I discovered through the accidents of biography a way to work that suggested the possibility of doing both in the poem at once.

Out of the accidental and haphazard can come something both magical and variously resonant with the life one leads, internally and in the world.

Note on the Author

Mark Weiss — art dealer, quondam film maker, psychotherapist and social worker, occasional teacher of writing, literature, film making, history and psychology — has published five books of poetry, most recently *Fieldnotes* (1995), from his own imprint, Junction Press, and *Figures: 32 Poems* (Chax Press, 2001). *Different Birds* appeared as an ebook in 2004 (Shearsman Books, http://www.shearsman.com/pages/books/ebooks/ebooks_home.html). He edited, with Harry Polkinhorn, the bilingual anthology *Across the Line / Al otro lado: The Poetry of Baja California* (Junction Press, 2002) and, with Marc Kaminsky, *Stories as Equipment for Living: Late Talks and Tales of Barbara Myerhoff* (University of Michigan Press, 2007). He translated and edited *Stet: Selected Poems of José Kozer* (Junction Press, 2006), *Cuaderno de San Antonio / The San Antonio Notebook*, by Javier Manríquez (La Paz, B.C.S., Mexico: Editorial Praxis, 2004), and *Notas del país de Z*, by Gaspar Orozco (Chihuahua: Universidad Autónoma de Chihuahua, 2008). His anthology *The Whole Island: Six Decades of Cuban Poetry* was published in 2009 by University of California Press. A native New Yorker, he has lived in Baltimore, Paris, Tucson, San Diego and rural Massachusetts. He currently lives at the edge of Manhattan's only forest.

About Chax Press

Chax Press was founded in 1984 as a creator of handmade fine arts editions of literature, often with an inventive and playful sense of how the book arts might interact with innovative writing. Beginning in 1990 the press started to publish works in trade paperback editions, such as the current book. We currently occupy studio space, shared with the painter Cynthia Miller, in the Small Planet Bakery building at the north side of downtown Tucson, Arizona. Recent books by Alice Notley, Barbara Henning, Charles Bernstein, Anne Waldman, Linh Dinh, Tenney Nathanson, and many more, may be found on our web site at chax.org.

Chax Press projects are supported by the Tucson Pima Arts Council, by the Arizona Commission on the Arts (with funding from the State of Arizona and the National Endowment for the Arts), by The Southwestern Foundation, and by many individual donors who keep us at work at the edges of contemporary literature through their generosity, friendship, and good spirits.

This book is set in Frederick Goudy's Old Style typeface in 11 point size, with titling in varying sizes, and some poem titling in Herman Zapf's Optima bold.
Composition and design in Adobe InDesign.
Cover photo: *The Lawn at Yaddo,* by Mark Weiss.